50 Winter Snowy Cooking Recipes

By: Kelly Johnson

Table of Contents

- Hot Chocolate
- Spiced Apple Cider
- Roasted Butternut Squash Soup
- Creamy Tomato Soup
- Beef Stew
- Chicken Pot Pie
- Mashed Potatoes with Gravy
- Baked Mac and Cheese
- Roasted Brussels Sprouts
- Roasted Root Vegetables
- Classic Meatloaf
- Chili Con Carne
- Baked Ziti
- Beef and Barley Soup
- Shepherd's Pie
- French Onion Soup
- Braised Short Ribs
- Pumpkin Soup
- Chicken Noodle Soup

- Pecan Pie
- Gingerbread Cookies
- Cinnamon Rolls
- Eggnog
- Hot Buttered Rum
- Molasses Cookies
- Cinnamon Sugar Donuts
- Chocolate Lava Cakes
- Apple Crisp
- Baked Apples with Cinnamon
- Sweet Potato Casserole
- Roasted Chicken with Vegetables
- Winter Salad with Pomegranate and Walnuts
- Garlic Parmesan Roasted Potatoes
- Snowman Pancakes
- Spiced Carrot Cake
- Cranberry Orange Muffins
- Roasted Chestnuts
- Snowball Cookies
- Pumpkin Bread
- White Chocolate Cranberry Cookies

- Baked Brie with Fig Jam
- Brown Butter Sage Pasta
- Hot Soup Dumplings
- Maple-Glazed Brussels Sprouts
- Spicy Lentil Soup
- Beef Wellington
- Braised Lamb Shanks
- Comforting Risotto
- Warm Apple Cider Donuts
- Peppermint Bark

Hot Chocolate

(A rich and creamy chocolate drink perfect for cozy nights)

Ingredients:

- 2 cups milk (or any milk alternative)
- 1/2 cup heavy cream
- 1/2 cup semisweet chocolate chips
- 1 tbsp cocoa powder
- 1 tbsp sugar (optional)
- 1/2 tsp vanilla extract
- Whipped cream and marshmallows (for topping)

Instructions:

1. **In a saucepan, heat the milk and cream** over medium heat until it starts to simmer (not boil).
2. **Whisk in the chocolate chips, cocoa powder, and sugar** until smooth and melted.
3. **Remove from heat** and stir in vanilla extract.
4. **Pour into mugs** and top with whipped cream and marshmallows.

Spiced Apple Cider

(A warm, spiced drink perfect for fall)

Ingredients:

- 4 cups apple cider
- 2 cinnamon sticks
- 4 cloves
- 1 star anise (optional)
- 1 orange, sliced
- 1 tbsp brown sugar (optional)

Instructions:

1. **In a saucepan, combine the apple cider, cinnamon sticks, cloves, star anise, and orange slices.**
2. **Bring to a simmer** over medium heat, then reduce the heat and let it simmer for about 10 minutes.
3. **Stir in brown sugar** if desired for added sweetness.
4. **Strain and serve hot.**

Roasted Butternut Squash Soup

(A creamy and hearty soup with a rich, nutty flavor)

Ingredients:

- 1 medium butternut squash, peeled, seeded, and cubed
- 1 onion, chopped
- 2 cloves garlic, minced
- 4 cups vegetable broth
- 1/2 cup coconut milk (or cream)
- 1 tbsp olive oil
- 1 tsp ground cinnamon
- Salt and pepper to taste

Instructions:

1. **Preheat the oven to 400°F (200°C).**
2. **Toss the butternut squash, onion, and garlic with olive oil, cinnamon, salt, and pepper.**
3. **Roast on a baking sheet** for 25-30 minutes, until tender.
4. **Transfer the roasted vegetables** to a blender and blend with the vegetable broth until smooth.
5. **Pour the soup into a pot**, stir in the coconut milk, and heat through.
6. **Serve hot.**

Creamy Tomato Soup

(A velvety tomato soup that's a perfect pairing with grilled cheese)

Ingredients:

- 1 can (28 oz) crushed tomatoes
- 1 onion, chopped
- 2 cloves garlic, minced
- 2 cups vegetable broth
- 1/2 cup heavy cream
- 1 tbsp olive oil
- 1 tsp dried basil
- Salt and pepper to taste

Instructions:

1. **Heat olive oil in a large pot** over medium heat. Add onion and garlic, and cook until softened.
2. **Add the crushed tomatoes, broth, and basil.** Stir and bring to a simmer.
3. **Simmer for 20 minutes** to let the flavors combine.
4. **Blend the soup** using an immersion blender until smooth.
5. **Stir in the heavy cream** and season with salt and pepper.
6. **Serve hot.**

Beef Stew

(A hearty stew with tender beef and vegetables)

Ingredients:

- 2 lbs beef chuck, cut into cubes
- 3 cups beef broth
- 4 carrots, peeled and sliced
- 3 potatoes, peeled and diced
- 1 onion, chopped
- 2 cloves garlic, minced
- 1 tbsp tomato paste
- 2 tbsp flour
- 1 tsp dried thyme
- 1 bay leaf
- Salt and pepper to taste

Instructions:

1. **In a large pot, brown the beef cubes** in some olive oil over medium heat, then set aside.
2. **In the same pot, sauté onion and garlic** until soft.
3. **Add the flour and tomato paste**, stirring for 1 minute.
4. **Add the broth, carrots, potatoes, beef, thyme, and bay leaf** to the pot. Stir to combine.
5. **Bring to a boil**, then reduce the heat and simmer for 1-1.5 hours, until the beef is tender.

6. **Season with salt and pepper** and serve hot.

Chicken Pot Pie

(A creamy and comforting chicken pie topped with flaky crust)

Ingredients:

- 2 cups cooked, shredded chicken
- 1 cup frozen peas and carrots
- 1/2 cup diced potatoes (optional)
- 1/2 cup butter
- 1/4 cup flour
- 2 cups chicken broth
- 1 cup milk
- 1 tsp thyme
- Salt and pepper to taste
- 1 pre-made pie crust (top and bottom)

Instructions:

1. **Preheat the oven to 375°F (190°C).**
2. **In a large saucepan, melt butter** over medium heat. Add flour and cook for 1-2 minutes.
3. **Slowly add the chicken broth and milk**, whisking until smooth and thickened.
4. **Stir in the chicken, vegetables, thyme, salt, and pepper.**
5. **Pour the mixture into a pie dish** and top with the pie crust.
6. **Cut slits in the top crust** and bake for 30-35 minutes, until golden brown.
7. **Let cool slightly before serving.**

Mashed Potatoes with Gravy

(A classic side dish with rich, flavorful gravy)

Ingredients for Mashed Potatoes:

- 4 large russet potatoes, peeled and cut into chunks
- 1/2 cup butter
- 1/2 cup milk
- Salt and pepper to taste

Ingredients for Gravy:

- 2 tbsp butter
- 2 tbsp flour
- 1 cup beef broth
- Salt and pepper to taste

Instructions:

1. **Boil the potatoes** in salted water until tender (about 15-20 minutes). Drain and mash with butter and milk. Season with salt and pepper.
2. **For the gravy, melt butter in a saucepan.** Stir in the flour and cook for 1-2 minutes.
3. **Gradually whisk in the beef broth**, and cook until thickened. Season with salt and pepper.
4. **Serve the mashed potatoes with gravy** on top.

Baked Mac and Cheese

(A creamy, cheesy baked pasta dish)

Ingredients:

- 1 lb elbow macaroni
- 2 cups shredded cheddar cheese
- 1 cup grated Parmesan cheese
- 1/2 cup breadcrumbs
- 1/4 cup butter
- 1/4 cup flour
- 2 cups milk
- 1 tsp Dijon mustard
- Salt and pepper to taste

Instructions:

1. **Cook the macaroni** according to the package directions. Drain and set aside.
2. **In a saucepan, melt butter**, stir in flour, and cook for 1-2 minutes.
3. **Slowly add milk** and cook until the sauce thickens. Stir in cheddar, Parmesan, and mustard. Season with salt and pepper.
4. **Combine the cooked macaroni with the cheese sauce** and transfer to a greased baking dish.
5. **Top with breadcrumbs** and bake at 350°F (175°C) for 20-25 minutes, until bubbly and golden.

Roasted Brussels Sprouts

(Simple and crispy Brussels sprouts with a little crunch)

Ingredients:

- 1 lb Brussels sprouts, trimmed and halved
- 2 tbsp olive oil
- Salt and pepper to taste

Instructions:

1. **Preheat oven to 400°F (200°C).**
2. **Toss Brussels sprouts** with olive oil, salt, and pepper.
3. **Roast on a baking sheet** for 25-30 minutes, shaking the pan halfway through.
4. **Serve hot.**

Roasted Root Vegetables

(A flavorful medley of root vegetables)

Ingredients:

- 2 carrots, peeled and cut into chunks
- 2 parsnips, peeled and cut into chunks
- 2 sweet potatoes, peeled and cut into chunks
- 1 tbsp olive oil
- Salt and pepper to taste
- 1 tsp rosemary

Instructions:

1. **Preheat oven to 400°F (200°C).**
2. **Toss vegetables** with olive oil, salt, pepper, and rosemary.
3. **Roast for 30-35 minutes**, until tender and caramelized.

Classic Meatloaf

(A hearty and classic comfort dish)

Ingredients:

- 1 lb ground beef
- 1 egg
- 1 cup breadcrumbs
- 1/4 cup milk
- 1/2 onion, chopped
- 1 tsp garlic powder
- 1/2 cup ketchup
- Salt and pepper to taste

Instructions:

1. **Preheat oven to 350°F (175°C).**
2. **Mix the ground beef, egg, breadcrumbs, milk, onion, garlic powder, ketchup, salt, and pepper** in a bowl.
3. **Shape the mixture into a loaf** and place in a greased baking dish.
4. **Top with ketchup** and bake for 50-60 minutes.
5. **Cool for a few minutes before slicing.**

Chili Con Carne

(A savory and spicy beef chili, perfect for cold nights)

Ingredients:

- 1 lb ground beef
- 1 onion, chopped
- 2 cloves garlic, minced
- 1 can (14 oz) diced tomatoes
- 1 can (15 oz) kidney beans, drained and rinsed
- 1 can (15 oz) black beans, drained and rinsed
- 1 can (6 oz) tomato paste
- 1 cup beef broth
- 2 tbsp chili powder
- 1 tsp cumin
- 1/2 tsp paprika
- Salt and pepper to taste
- 1/4 cup shredded cheddar cheese (optional, for topping)

Instructions:

1. **Brown the ground beef** in a large pot over medium heat, breaking it up into small pieces.
2. **Add the chopped onion and minced garlic** and cook until softened.
3. **Stir in the diced tomatoes, beans, tomato paste, and beef broth**.
4. **Add the chili powder, cumin, paprika, salt, and pepper**. Stir to combine.

5. **Simmer for 30-45 minutes**, stirring occasionally.

6. **Serve hot** with shredded cheddar cheese on top, if desired.

Baked Ziti

(A cheesy, baked pasta dish that's sure to satisfy)

Ingredients:

- 1 lb ziti pasta
- 1 jar (24 oz) marinara sauce
- 2 cups ricotta cheese
- 2 cups shredded mozzarella cheese
- 1/2 cup grated Parmesan cheese
- 1 egg
- 2 tbsp fresh basil, chopped
- Salt and pepper to taste

Instructions:

1. **Preheat oven to 375°F (190°C).**
2. **Cook the ziti pasta** according to package directions, then drain and set aside.
3. **In a bowl, mix ricotta cheese, egg, basil, salt, and pepper.**
4. **Combine the cooked pasta, marinara sauce, ricotta mixture, and half of the mozzarella cheese.**
5. **Transfer the mixture to a baking dish** and top with the remaining mozzarella and Parmesan cheese.
6. **Bake for 25-30 minutes** until the cheese is melted and bubbly.
7. **Serve hot.**

Beef and Barley Soup

(A hearty, healthy soup with tender beef and nutritious barley)

Ingredients:

- 1 lb beef stew meat, cubed
- 1 onion, chopped
- 2 carrots, sliced
- 2 celery stalks, chopped
- 1 cup pearl barley
- 6 cups beef broth
- 2 cloves garlic, minced
- 1 tsp dried thyme
- Salt and pepper to taste

Instructions:

1. **In a large pot, brown the beef stew meat** over medium heat, then set aside.
2. **Add the onion, carrots, and celery** to the pot and sauté until softened.
3. **Stir in the garlic and cook for 1 minute** until fragrant.
4. **Add the beef broth, barley, thyme, and browned beef.**
5. **Bring to a boil, then reduce heat and simmer for 1-1.5 hours** until the beef is tender and barley is cooked.
6. **Season with salt and pepper** and serve hot.

Shepherd's Pie

(A classic comfort dish with ground meat and mashed potatoes)

Ingredients:

- 1 lb ground beef or lamb
- 1 onion, chopped
- 2 cloves garlic, minced
- 2 carrots, diced
- 1/2 cup peas
- 2 cups mashed potatoes
- 1/2 cup beef broth
- 1 tbsp Worcestershire sauce
- 2 tbsp flour
- Salt and pepper to taste

Instructions:

1. **Preheat oven to 400°F (200°C).**
2. **Cook the ground beef or lamb** in a skillet until browned, then remove excess fat.
3. **Add the onion, garlic, and carrots**, and cook until softened.
4. **Stir in the flour** and cook for 1-2 minutes.
5. **Add the beef broth and Worcestershire sauce**, stirring until thickened.
6. **Add the peas**, season with salt and pepper, and mix well.
7. **Transfer the mixture into a baking dish** and top with mashed potatoes.
8. **Bake for 20 minutes**, or until the top is golden brown.

9. **Serve hot.**

French Onion Soup

(A rich, savory soup topped with melted cheese and toasted bread)

Ingredients:

- 4 large onions, thinly sliced
- 2 tbsp butter
- 1 tbsp olive oil
- 4 cups beef broth
- 1/2 cup white wine (optional)
- 1 tsp dried thyme
- Salt and pepper to taste
- 4 slices French baguette
- 2 cups shredded Gruyère cheese

Instructions:

1. **In a large pot, melt butter and olive oil** over medium heat. Add the onions and cook, stirring occasionally, for 30-40 minutes until caramelized.
2. **Add the wine (if using), beef broth, thyme, salt, and pepper**. Bring to a boil, then reduce heat and simmer for 10 minutes.
3. **Meanwhile, toast the baguette slices** until golden brown.
4. **Ladle the soup into bowls**, top with a slice of toasted baguette, and sprinkle with Gruyère cheese.
5. **Broil the soup** in the oven for 3-5 minutes, until the cheese is melted and bubbly.
6. **Serve hot.**

Braised Short Ribs

(Tender, fall-off-the-bone short ribs with a rich sauce)

Ingredients:

- 4-6 bone-in short ribs
- 2 tbsp olive oil
- 1 onion, chopped
- 2 carrots, chopped
- 2 cloves garlic, minced
- 2 cups beef broth
- 1 cup red wine
- 2 tbsp tomato paste
- 1 tbsp fresh rosemary, chopped
- Salt and pepper to taste

Instructions:

1. **Preheat oven to 325°F (165°C).**
2. **Brown the short ribs** in olive oil over medium-high heat. Remove and set aside.
3. **In the same pot, sauté the onion, carrots, and garlic** until softened.
4. **Add the tomato paste**, stirring for 1-2 minutes.
5. **Pour in the wine and beef broth**, scraping the bottom of the pot.
6. **Return the short ribs to the pot**, add rosemary, salt, and pepper.
7. **Cover and braise in the oven** for 2-3 hours, until the ribs are tender.
8. **Serve hot.**

Pumpkin Soup

(A creamy and savory soup with the warmth of pumpkin)

Ingredients:

- 1 can (15 oz) pure pumpkin
- 1 onion, chopped
- 2 cloves garlic, minced
- 4 cups vegetable broth
- 1/2 cup heavy cream
- 1 tsp ground cinnamon
- 1/2 tsp nutmeg
- Salt and pepper to taste

Instructions:

1. **In a large pot, sauté the onion and garlic** in olive oil until softened.
2. **Add the pumpkin, broth, cinnamon, nutmeg, salt, and pepper**.
3. **Bring to a boil**, then reduce heat and simmer for 15-20 minutes.
4. **Blend the soup** using an immersion blender until smooth.
5. **Stir in the heavy cream**, heat through, and serve hot.

Chicken Noodle Soup

(A classic, comforting soup with tender chicken and noodles)

Ingredients:

- 2 chicken breasts, cooked and shredded
- 2 carrots, sliced
- 2 celery stalks, chopped
- 1 onion, chopped
- 4 cups chicken broth
- 1 cup egg noodles
- 2 cloves garlic, minced
- 1 tsp dried thyme
- Salt and pepper to taste

Instructions:

1. **In a large pot, sauté the onion, garlic, carrots, and celery** until softened.
2. **Add the chicken broth, shredded chicken, thyme, salt, and pepper**. Bring to a boil.
3. **Add the egg noodles** and cook for 8-10 minutes, until the noodles are tender.
4. **Serve hot.**

Pecan Pie

(A rich and sweet pie filled with pecans and syrup)

Ingredients:

- 1 1/2 cups pecans
- 1 cup corn syrup
- 1/2 cup brown sugar
- 1/4 cup butter, melted
- 3 large eggs
- 1 tsp vanilla extract
- 1/4 tsp salt
- 1 pie crust (store-bought or homemade)

Instructions:

1. **Preheat oven to 350°F (175°C).**
2. **In a bowl, whisk together the corn syrup, brown sugar, melted butter, eggs, vanilla, and salt.**
3. **Stir in the pecans** and pour the mixture into the pie crust.
4. **Bake for 50-60 minutes**, until set. Let cool before serving.

Gingerbread Cookies

(Sweet and spiced cookies, perfect for the holidays)

Ingredients:

- 2 1/4 cups all-purpose flour
- 1/2 tsp baking soda
- 1 tbsp ground ginger
- 1 tbsp ground cinnamon
- 1/2 tsp ground cloves
- 1/4 tsp salt
- 3/4 cup unsalted butter, softened
- 1/2 cup brown sugar
- 1 egg
- 1/2 cup molasses

Instructions:

1. **Preheat oven to 350°F (175°C).**
2. **In a bowl, whisk together the flour, baking soda, spices, and salt.**
3. **In another bowl, cream the butter and brown sugar**, then add the egg and molasses.
4. **Gradually add the dry ingredients** to the wet mixture and mix until combined.
5. **Roll the dough into balls** and place on a baking sheet.
6. **Bake for 8-10 minutes**, until the edges are firm. Let cool before serving.

Cinnamon Rolls

(Fluffy, warm cinnamon rolls topped with cream cheese icing)

Ingredients for the Dough:

- 2 1/4 tsp active dry yeast
- 1 cup warm milk
- 1/2 cup sugar
- 1/2 cup melted butter
- 1 tsp salt
- 2 eggs
- 4 cups all-purpose flour

Ingredients for the Filling:

- 1/2 cup butter, softened
- 1 cup brown sugar
- 2 tbsp ground cinnamon
- 1/2 tsp ground nutmeg

Ingredients for the Icing:

- 4 oz cream cheese, softened
- 1 cup powdered sugar
- 1 tsp vanilla extract
- 2 tbsp milk

Instructions:

1. **For the dough**, mix warm milk and yeast in a bowl and let it sit for 5-10 minutes until foamy.

2. Add sugar, melted butter, salt, eggs, and flour. Mix until a dough forms, then knead on a floured surface for 5 minutes.

3. Let the dough rise in a warm place for 1-2 hours, or until doubled in size.

4. Preheat oven to 350°F (175°C).

5. Roll the dough into a large rectangle. Spread softened butter, sprinkle cinnamon sugar, and then roll it up tightly.

6. Slice into rolls and place in a greased baking dish.

7. Bake for 20-25 minutes.

8. **For the icing**, mix all ingredients until smooth, then drizzle over the warm rolls.

9. Serve fresh and enjoy!

Eggnog

(A classic, creamy holiday drink)

Ingredients:

- 4 large eggs
- 1 cup sugar
- 2 cups milk
- 1 cup heavy cream
- 1/2 cup bourbon or rum (optional)
- 1/2 tsp ground nutmeg
- 1 tsp vanilla extract
- Freshly grated nutmeg, for garnish

Instructions:

1. **Whisk the eggs and sugar** in a bowl until smooth.
2. In a saucepan, heat milk and cream over medium heat until warm but not boiling.
3. Gradually pour the warm milk mixture into the egg mixture, whisking constantly.
4. Return to the saucepan and cook over low heat, stirring constantly, until it thickens slightly (about 5-7 minutes).
5. Stir in the alcohol, nutmeg, and vanilla extract.
6. **Chill the eggnog** in the refrigerator for at least 2 hours.
7. Serve cold, garnished with freshly grated nutmeg.

Hot Buttered Rum

(A rich and indulgent winter drink)

Ingredients:

- 2 oz dark rum
- 1 tbsp butter
- 1 tbsp brown sugar
- 1/4 tsp ground cinnamon
- 1/4 tsp ground nutmeg
- 1 cup hot water

Instructions:

1. **Melt butter** with brown sugar, cinnamon, and nutmeg in a mug.
2. Add dark rum and hot water, stirring until the sugar is dissolved and everything is well combined.
3. **Serve hot** and enjoy the cozy warmth!

Molasses Cookies

(Soft, chewy cookies with warm spices)

Ingredients:

- 2 1/4 cups all-purpose flour
- 2 tsp ground ginger
- 1 tsp ground cinnamon
- 1/2 tsp ground cloves
- 1/2 tsp baking soda
- 1/4 tsp salt
- 3/4 cup unsalted butter, softened
- 1 cup brown sugar
- 1/4 cup molasses
- 1 large egg
- Sugar for rolling (optional)

Instructions:

1. **Preheat oven to 350°F (175°C).**
2. In a bowl, whisk together flour, ginger, cinnamon, cloves, baking soda, and salt.
3. In a separate bowl, beat together butter and brown sugar until creamy. Add molasses and egg, then mix until smooth.
4. Gradually add the dry ingredients to the wet mixture, mixing until combined.
5. Roll dough into 1-inch balls and roll in sugar (optional).
6. Place on a baking sheet and bake for 8-10 minutes, until edges are firm.

7. Cool on a wire rack and enjoy!

Cinnamon Sugar Donuts

(Fried donuts with a sweet cinnamon coating)

Ingredients for the Donuts:

- 2 cups all-purpose flour
- 1/2 cup sugar
- 2 tsp baking powder
- 1/2 tsp ground cinnamon
- 1/4 tsp salt
- 2 large eggs
- 3/4 cup milk
- 1/4 cup melted butter
- Vegetable oil for frying

Ingredients for the Coating:

- 1/2 cup sugar
- 1 tbsp ground cinnamon

Instructions:

1. **Preheat oil in a deep fryer or large pot** to 350°F (175°C).
2. In a large bowl, combine flour, sugar, baking powder, cinnamon, and salt.
3. In a separate bowl, whisk together eggs, milk, and melted butter. Add to the dry ingredients and stir to combine.
4. **Scoop the dough** into a donut pan or roll into balls and fry. Fry until golden brown (2-3 minutes), then drain on paper towels.

5. **Mix sugar and cinnamon** in a bowl and roll the warm donuts in the mixture.

6. Serve fresh and enjoy!

Chocolate Lava Cakes

(Decadent chocolate cakes with a molten center)

Ingredients:

- 1/2 cup unsalted butter
- 6 oz semisweet chocolate
- 1/4 cup sugar
- 2 large eggs
- 2 large egg yolks
- 1 tsp vanilla extract
- 1/4 cup all-purpose flour

Instructions:

1. **Preheat oven to 425°F (220°C).**
2. Grease 4 ramekins with butter and lightly dust with flour.
3. **Melt butter and chocolate** in a bowl over a double boiler or in the microwave. Stir until smooth.
4. In a separate bowl, whisk together eggs, egg yolks, sugar, and vanilla until smooth.
5. **Combine the chocolate mixture** with the egg mixture and stir in flour until smooth.
6. Pour the batter evenly into the prepared ramekins.
7. **Bake for 12-14 minutes**, until the edges are set but the center is still soft.
8. Let rest for 1 minute, then carefully run a knife around the edges and invert onto plates.
9. Serve warm with a scoop of vanilla ice cream.

Apple Crisp

(A warm, comforting dessert with baked apples and a crumbly topping)

Ingredients for the Filling:

- 6 cups apples, peeled and sliced
- 1/4 cup sugar
- 1 tbsp lemon juice
- 1 tsp ground cinnamon
- 1/4 tsp salt

Ingredients for the Topping:

- 1 cup oats
- 1/2 cup flour
- 1/2 cup brown sugar
- 1/2 cup butter, melted
- 1/2 tsp ground cinnamon

Instructions:

1. **Preheat oven to 350°F (175°C).**
2. In a large bowl, combine apples with sugar, lemon juice, cinnamon, and salt. Transfer to a greased baking dish.
3. In a separate bowl, mix oats, flour, brown sugar, butter, and cinnamon. Sprinkle evenly over the apples.
4. **Bake for 40-45 minutes** until the topping is golden brown and the apples are tender.
5. Serve warm with whipped cream or vanilla ice cream.

Baked Apples with Cinnamon

(Simple and healthy dessert with a warm, spiced apple filling)

Ingredients:

- 4 medium apples (Granny Smith or Honeycrisp work well)
- 1/4 cup brown sugar
- 1 tsp ground cinnamon
- 1/4 cup chopped walnuts or raisins (optional)
- 1/4 cup butter
- 1/4 cup water

Instructions:

1. **Preheat oven to 350°F (175°C).**
2. Core the apples and place them in a baking dish.
3. Mix brown sugar, cinnamon, and walnuts/raisins (if using). Stuff the mixture into the center of each apple.
4. Place a small pat of butter on top of each apple and pour water into the bottom of the baking dish.
5. **Bake for 30-35 minutes**, until the apples are tender.
6. Serve warm with a scoop of vanilla ice cream or whipped cream.

Sweet Potato Casserole

(A creamy and sweet casserole, topped with a buttery streusel)

Ingredients for the Filling:

- 4 large sweet potatoes, peeled and cubed
- 1/2 cup sugar
- 1/4 cup milk
- 1/4 cup melted butter
- 2 eggs
- 1 tsp vanilla extract
- 1/2 tsp ground cinnamon

Ingredients for the Topping:

- 1/2 cup brown sugar
- 1/4 cup flour
- 1/4 cup melted butter
- 1/2 cup chopped pecans

Instructions:

1. **Preheat oven to 350°F (175°C).**
2. Boil the sweet potatoes until tender, then mash them.
3. Stir in sugar, milk, butter, eggs, vanilla, and cinnamon until smooth.
4. Transfer to a greased baking dish.
5. In a separate bowl, mix brown sugar, flour, butter, and pecans for the topping. Sprinkle over the sweet potato mixture.

6. **Bake for 25-30 minutes** until golden and bubbly.

7. Serve warm and enjoy!

Roasted Chicken with Vegetables

(A comforting and hearty one-pan meal)

Ingredients:

- 1 whole chicken (3-4 lbs)
- 1 tbsp olive oil
- 1 tbsp fresh rosemary, chopped
- 1 tbsp thyme leaves
- 2 cloves garlic, minced
- Salt and pepper to taste
- 4 medium carrots, peeled and cut into sticks
- 4 medium potatoes, cut into chunks
- 1 large onion, quartered
- 2 tbsp butter
- 1 lemon, halved

Instructions:

1. **Preheat oven to 425°F (220°C).**
2. Pat the chicken dry and rub with olive oil, rosemary, thyme, garlic, salt, and pepper.
3. Stuff the chicken cavity with lemon halves and additional rosemary or thyme.
4. In a large roasting pan, arrange the carrots, potatoes, and onion. Place the chicken on top.
5. Dot the vegetables with butter and season with salt and pepper.
6. **Roast for 1 hour and 20 minutes**, or until the chicken reaches an internal temperature of 165°F (75°C) and the vegetables are tender.

7. Let the chicken rest for 10 minutes before carving. Serve the chicken with roasted vegetables.

Winter Salad with Pomegranate and Walnuts

(Fresh and colorful salad perfect for the holidays)

Ingredients:

- 4 cups mixed greens (arugula, spinach, or kale)
- 1/2 cup pomegranate seeds
- 1/4 cup toasted walnuts
- 1/4 cup crumbled feta cheese
- 1/2 red onion, thinly sliced
- 1/4 cup balsamic vinaigrette

Instructions:

1. In a large bowl, combine the mixed greens, pomegranate seeds, walnuts, feta, and red onion.
2. Drizzle with balsamic vinaigrette and toss gently.
3. Serve immediately as a fresh side dish.

Garlic Parmesan Roasted Potatoes

(Crispy, savory potatoes with garlic and Parmesan)

Ingredients:

- 1 lb baby potatoes, halved
- 3 tbsp olive oil
- 3 cloves garlic, minced
- 1/2 cup grated Parmesan cheese
- 1 tbsp fresh parsley, chopped
- Salt and pepper to taste

Instructions:

1. **Preheat oven to 400°F (200°C).**
2. In a bowl, toss the halved potatoes with olive oil, garlic, salt, and pepper.
3. Spread the potatoes on a baking sheet in a single layer.
4. **Roast for 25-30 minutes**, turning halfway through, until golden and crispy.
5. Remove from the oven and sprinkle with Parmesan and fresh parsley. Serve hot.

Snowman Pancakes

(Fun and festive pancakes for the holidays)

Ingredients:

- 1 1/2 cups pancake mix
- 1 cup milk
- 1 egg
- 1 tbsp melted butter
- Chocolate chips (for eyes and buttons)
- A slice of orange (for the nose)
- Whipped cream (for snow)

Instructions:

1. **Prepare the pancake batter** according to the package directions, adding milk, egg, and melted butter.
2. Heat a griddle or skillet over medium heat and lightly grease with cooking spray.
3. Pour the batter in circles, starting with larger ones for the body and a smaller one for the head. Cook until golden brown on both sides.
4. Stack the pancakes to form a snowman shape, with the large pancake on the bottom and the smaller one on top.
5. Decorate with chocolate chips for eyes and buttons, an orange slice for the nose, and whipped cream for snow.
6. Serve with maple syrup or fruit.

Spiced Carrot Cake

(A moist and flavorful carrot cake with warm spices)

Ingredients for the Cake:

- 2 cups all-purpose flour
- 1 tsp baking soda
- 1/2 tsp baking powder
- 1/2 tsp salt
- 1 tsp ground cinnamon
- 1/2 tsp ground nutmeg
- 4 large eggs
- 1 1/2 cups sugar
- 1 cup vegetable oil
- 2 cups grated carrots
- 1/2 cup chopped walnuts (optional)
- 1/2 cup raisins (optional)

Ingredients for the Frosting:

- 8 oz cream cheese, softened
- 1/4 cup unsalted butter, softened
- 2 cups powdered sugar
- 1 tsp vanilla extract

Instructions:

1. **Preheat oven to 350°F (175°C).** Grease and flour a 9x13-inch baking pan.

2. In a medium bowl, whisk together the flour, baking soda, baking powder, salt, cinnamon, and nutmeg.

3. In a large bowl, beat together the eggs and sugar until smooth. Gradually add the oil and beat until combined.

4. Stir in the grated carrots, walnuts, and raisins (if using).

5. Add the dry ingredients to the wet ingredients and mix until just combined.

6. **Pour the batter into the prepared pan** and bake for 30-35 minutes, or until a toothpick comes out clean.

7. While the cake is cooling, beat the cream cheese and butter together until smooth. Gradually add the powdered sugar and vanilla, and beat until fluffy.

8. Frost the cooled cake and serve.

Cranberry Orange Muffins

(Fresh muffins with tangy cranberries and citrus flavor)

Ingredients:

- 2 cups all-purpose flour
- 1 cup sugar
- 2 tsp baking powder
- 1/2 tsp baking soda
- 1/2 tsp salt
- 1/2 tsp ground cinnamon
- 1/2 cup buttermilk
- 1/4 cup vegetable oil
- 1 large egg
- Zest of 1 orange
- 1 cup fresh cranberries, chopped (or frozen)

Instructions:

1. **Preheat oven to 350°F (175°C).** Line a muffin tin with paper liners.
2. In a large bowl, whisk together the flour, sugar, baking powder, baking soda, salt, and cinnamon.
3. In a separate bowl, whisk together the buttermilk, oil, egg, and orange zest.
4. Add the wet ingredients to the dry ingredients and stir until just combined. Gently fold in the cranberries.
5. **Spoon the batter** into the muffin cups, filling each about 2/3 full.
6. Bake for 18-20 minutes, or until a toothpick comes out clean.

7. Cool on a wire rack and enjoy.

Roasted Chestnuts

(A simple, seasonal snack)

Ingredients:

- 1 lb chestnuts (fresh, not pre-packaged)

Instructions:

1. **Preheat oven to 400°F (200°C).**
2. Cut an "X" into the flat side of each chestnut using a sharp knife.
3. Place the chestnuts on a baking sheet, cut side up.
4. **Roast for 20-30 minutes**, shaking the pan halfway through.
5. Once cool enough to handle, peel the shells and enjoy the warm, nutty treat!

Snowball Cookies

(Buttery, melt-in-your-mouth cookies rolled in powdered sugar)

Ingredients:

- 1 cup unsalted butter, softened
- 1/4 cup powdered sugar, plus extra for rolling
- 1 tsp vanilla extract
- 2 cups all-purpose flour
- 1/4 tsp salt
- 1 cup chopped nuts (optional)

Instructions:

1. **Preheat oven to 350°F (175°C).** Line a baking sheet with parchment paper.
2. Beat the butter and powdered sugar together until smooth. Add the vanilla extract.
3. Gradually add the flour and salt, mixing until combined. Fold in the nuts if using.
4. Roll dough into 1-inch balls and place on the baking sheet.
5. **Bake for 10-12 minutes**, or until the cookies are lightly golden on the bottom.
6. While warm, roll the cookies in powdered sugar.
7. Cool completely before serving.

Pumpkin Bread

(A moist and spiced pumpkin loaf perfect for fall and winter)

Ingredients:

- 1 3/4 cups all-purpose flour
- 1 tsp baking soda
- 1/2 tsp salt
- 1/2 tsp ground cinnamon
- 1/2 tsp ground nutmeg
- 1/2 tsp ground ginger
- 1 cup sugar
- 1/2 cup vegetable oil
- 2 large eggs
- 1 1/2 cups canned pumpkin puree
- 1 tsp vanilla extract

Instructions:

1. **Preheat oven to 350°F (175°C).** Grease and flour a loaf pan.
2. In a large bowl, whisk together the flour, baking soda, salt, cinnamon, nutmeg, and ginger.
3. In a separate bowl, whisk together the sugar, oil, eggs, pumpkin, and vanilla.
4. Gradually add the wet ingredients to the dry ingredients, mixing until just combined.
5. **Pour the batter into the prepared pan** and bake for 60-70 minutes, or until a toothpick comes out clean.
6. Let cool in the pan for 10 minutes before transferring to a wire rack. Slice and serve.

White Chocolate Cranberry Cookies

(A sweet and tart cookie with creamy white chocolate and tangy cranberries)

Ingredients:

- 1 cup unsalted butter, softened
- 1 cup brown sugar
- 1/2 cup granulated sugar
- 2 large eggs
- 1 tsp vanilla extract
- 2 1/2 cups all-purpose flour
- 1 tsp baking soda
- 1/2 tsp salt
- 1 1/2 cups dried cranberries
- 1 cup white chocolate chips

Instructions:

1. **Preheat oven to 350°F (175°C).** Line a baking sheet with parchment paper.
2. Cream together the butter, brown sugar, and granulated sugar until smooth.
3. Add the eggs and vanilla extract, mixing until combined.
4. In a separate bowl, whisk together the flour, baking soda, and salt. Gradually add to the wet ingredients.
5. Stir in the cranberries and white chocolate chips.
6. **Scoop the dough** onto the prepared baking sheet in tablespoon-sized portions.
7. Bake for 10-12 minutes, or until golden around the edges.

8. Cool on a wire rack before serving.

Baked Brie with Fig Jam

(A savory, gooey Brie topped with sweet fig jam, baked until perfectly melted)

Ingredients:

- 1 wheel of Brie cheese (8 oz)
- 2 tbsp fig jam
- 1/4 cup chopped walnuts (optional)
- Fresh thyme (optional)
- Crackers or baguette slices, for serving

Instructions:

1. **Preheat oven to 350°F (175°C).**
2. Place the Brie on a small baking dish or oven-safe skillet.
3. Top with fig jam and sprinkle with walnuts and thyme if desired.
4. **Bake for 10-12 minutes** or until the Brie is soft and melted.
5. Serve with crackers or sliced baguette.

Brown Butter Sage Pasta

(A rich, nutty brown butter sauce with crispy sage leaves over pasta)

Ingredients:

- 12 oz pasta (such as fettuccine or spaghetti)
- 1/2 cup unsalted butter
- 1/2 cup fresh sage leaves
- 1/2 cup grated Parmesan cheese
- Salt and pepper to taste

Instructions:

1. **Cook pasta** according to package directions. Reserve 1/2 cup of pasta water before draining.
2. In a large pan, melt the butter over medium heat. Let it cook, swirling occasionally, until it turns golden brown and has a nutty aroma.
3. Add the fresh sage leaves and cook until crispy, about 1-2 minutes.
4. Add the cooked pasta to the pan, tossing to coat. If the sauce is too thick, add reserved pasta water, one tablespoon at a time.
5. Stir in grated Parmesan cheese and season with salt and pepper.
6. Serve immediately.

Hot Soup Dumplings

(Savory dumplings filled with a flavorful broth that bursts when bitten)

Ingredients:

- 1 lb ground pork
- 2 tbsp soy sauce
- 1 tbsp sesame oil
- 1 tbsp ginger, minced
- 1/2 cup chicken stock
- 1/4 cup scallions, chopped
- Dumpling wrappers
- 1 tbsp cornstarch (to thicken broth)

Instructions:

1. In a bowl, combine ground pork, soy sauce, sesame oil, ginger, and scallions.
2. In a small saucepan, heat the chicken stock until simmering, then mix in the cornstarch. Cook until it thickens to a jelly-like consistency. Let it cool slightly.
3. Place a spoonful of the pork mixture and a small teaspoon of the broth inside each dumpling wrapper. Fold and seal the dumplings tightly.
4. **Steam the dumplings** over simmering water for 8-10 minutes, or until the wrappers are translucent and the filling is cooked through.
5. Serve hot with soy sauce or vinegar.

Maple-Glazed Brussels Sprouts

(A sweet and savory side dish with crispy Brussels sprouts coated in maple syrup)

Ingredients:

- 1 lb Brussels sprouts, halved
- 2 tbsp olive oil
- Salt and pepper to taste
- 1/4 cup maple syrup
- 1 tbsp balsamic vinegar

Instructions:

1. **Preheat oven to 400°F (200°C).**
2. Toss the halved Brussels sprouts with olive oil, salt, and pepper.
3. Spread them in a single layer on a baking sheet and roast for 20-25 minutes, flipping halfway, until crispy.
4. While the Brussels sprouts roast, mix the maple syrup and balsamic vinegar in a small saucepan and simmer for 2-3 minutes.
5. Drizzle the maple glaze over the roasted Brussels sprouts and toss to coat. Serve warm.

Spicy Lentil Soup

(A hearty, spicy soup with lentils, tomatoes, and warming spices)

Ingredients:

- 1 tbsp olive oil
- 1 onion, chopped
- 2 cloves garlic, minced
- 1 carrot, chopped
- 1 celery stalk, chopped
- 1 tbsp ground cumin
- 1 tbsp ground coriander
- 1 tsp smoked paprika
- 1 1/2 cups red lentils
- 1 can (14 oz) diced tomatoes
- 4 cups vegetable broth
- Salt and pepper to taste
- Fresh cilantro, for garnish

Instructions:

1. In a large pot, heat olive oil over medium heat. Add the onion, garlic, carrot, and celery and sauté for 5 minutes.
2. Stir in cumin, coriander, and paprika, and cook for another minute.
3. Add the lentils, diced tomatoes, vegetable broth, salt, and pepper. Bring to a simmer and cook for 25-30 minutes, or until the lentils are tender.

4. Puree half of the soup using an immersion blender or by transferring it to a blender (optional for a smoother texture).

5. Garnish with fresh cilantro and serve.

Beef Wellington

(A luxurious dish with beef tenderloin wrapped in prosciutto, mushrooms, and puff pastry)

Ingredients:

- 1 lb beef tenderloin
- 2 tbsp olive oil
- Salt and pepper
- 1/2 lb mushrooms, finely chopped
- 2 tbsp Dijon mustard
- 4 oz prosciutto
- 1 sheet puff pastry
- 1 egg, beaten

Instructions:

1. **Preheat oven to 400°F (200°C).**
2. Season the beef tenderloin with salt and pepper. Heat olive oil in a skillet over high heat and sear the beef on all sides until browned, about 5-7 minutes. Let it cool and brush with Dijon mustard.
3. In the same skillet, sauté the mushrooms until they release their moisture and become dry. Let cool.
4. Lay out the prosciutto on a piece of plastic wrap, then spread the mushrooms over the prosciutto. Place the beef on top and roll it up tightly.
5. Roll out the puff pastry and wrap the beef tightly in the pastry. Seal the edges and brush with the beaten egg.
6. **Bake for 25-30 minutes** or until the pastry is golden and crisp. Let it rest before slicing.

Braised Lamb Shanks

(Tender, slow-cooked lamb shanks in a rich, flavorful broth)

Ingredients:

- 2 lamb shanks
- 2 tbsp olive oil
- Salt and pepper to taste
- 1 onion, chopped
- 2 carrots, chopped
- 2 cloves garlic, minced
- 1 cup red wine
- 2 cups beef broth
- 1 sprig rosemary
- 2 sprigs thyme

Instructions:

1. **Preheat oven to 325°F (165°C).**
2. Season the lamb shanks with salt and pepper. Heat olive oil in a large pot and sear the shanks on all sides. Remove and set aside.
3. In the same pot, sauté onion, carrots, and garlic until softened, about 5 minutes.
4. Add the wine, scraping up any browned bits, and bring to a simmer. Add the beef broth, rosemary, and thyme.
5. Return the lamb shanks to the pot and cover. Braise in the oven for 2-3 hours, until the lamb is tender.
6. Serve with the braising liquid spooned over the top.

Comforting Risotto

(A creamy rice dish with Parmesan and butter)

Ingredients:

- 1 cup Arborio rice
- 1 tbsp olive oil
- 1 small onion, chopped
- 2 cloves garlic, minced
- 4 cups chicken or vegetable broth, warm
- 1/2 cup dry white wine
- 1/2 cup grated Parmesan cheese
- 2 tbsp butter
- Salt and pepper to taste

Instructions:

1. In a large pan, heat olive oil over medium heat. Add the onion and garlic and cook until softened, about 5 minutes.

2. Add the rice and stir until the grains are well-coated.

3. Pour in the wine and stir until absorbed. Gradually add the warm broth, one ladle at a time, stirring constantly and allowing the liquid to absorb before adding more. Continue until the rice is tender and creamy, about 20-25 minutes.

4. Stir in Parmesan cheese, butter, salt, and pepper. Serve warm.

Warm Apple Cider Donuts

(Sweet and fluffy apple cider donuts with a hint of spice)

Ingredients:

- 2 cups all-purpose flour
- 1 tsp baking powder
- 1/2 tsp baking soda
- 1/2 tsp cinnamon
- 1/4 tsp nutmeg
- 1/2 tsp salt
- 1/2 cup brown sugar
- 1/2 cup apple cider
- 2 tbsp unsalted butter, melted
- 1 egg
- 1 tsp vanilla extract
- Cinnamon sugar, for coating

Instructions:

1. **Preheat oven to 375°F (190°C).** Grease a donut pan.
2. In a bowl, whisk together the flour, baking powder, baking soda, cinnamon, nutmeg, and salt.
3. In another bowl, combine the brown sugar, apple cider, melted butter, egg, and vanilla extract. Add the dry ingredients and stir until combined.
4. Pour the batter into the donut pan, filling each cup about 3/4 full.
5. **Bake for 12-15 minutes** or until a toothpick comes out clean.

6. Roll the warm donuts in cinnamon sugar and serve.

Peppermint Bark

(A festive, minty chocolate treat)

Ingredients:

- 8 oz white chocolate
- 8 oz dark chocolate
- 1/2 tsp peppermint extract
- 1/2 cup crushed peppermint candies

Instructions:

1. **Melt the dark chocolate** in a double boiler or microwave. Spread it in an even layer on a parchment-lined baking sheet.
2. **Melt the white chocolate** in the same way, then stir in peppermint extract. Pour the white chocolate over the dark chocolate and swirl gently to create a marbled effect.
3. Sprinkle the crushed peppermint candies over the top.
4. Let the bark cool and harden at room temperature, then break into pieces.

www.ingramcontent.com/pod-product-compliance
Lightning Source LLC
LaVergne TN
LVHW081318060526
838201LV00055B/2347